Baptized in Muddy Water

Based on a true story

C. L. Whitley

NEWMAN SPRINGS PUBLISHING
320 Broad Street
Red Bank, NJ 07701

First originally published by Newman Springs Publishing 2024

ISBN 979-8-89308-541-9 (Paperback)
ISBN 979-8-89308-542-6 (Digital)

Printed in the United States of America

These are stories about growing up in a family of bootleggers and connections to the Dixie Mafia.

We all have paths in this life; some we choose, some are chosen for us.

In loving memory of dad.

THIS STORY IS about a man born and raised in the South. His story really began back when he was about nine or maybe ten years old. He had two other brothers. The boys got into all kinds of mischief. Which was easy because at that time their father worked on the Illinois Central Railroad.

They lived in camps of canvas huts, so when the trains moved, they moved. These camps always provided stores for supplies for schools and churches.

Their mother made sure they were at school and church. Most of the time, the boys were left to find their own entertainment like playing with a ten-pound snapping turtle before taking it to Mother to cook.

But on Sunday mornings, she had them in church. But in all her efforts, she could not control James, her middle child. Even her prayers seem to go unanswered. This young man was just too high-strung and too hot-tempered. She would soon find out.

One bright, sunny Sunday morning, while they were sitting in church, she made sure the boys sat beside her. Well, unknown to her, an unsupervised boy sitting behind James was restless, to say the least, until he kicked the back of his seat, pulled his hair, and thumped his head. When James turned around to confront the boy, his mother wasn't having it. She would slap James on the knee to make him turn around and pay attention. But the boy wouldn't stop.

James just couldn't take any more. Mother, hearing the commotion, went outside. Her sweet son had cut the other kid with a small pocket knife he carried in his pocket. The other boy was fine, but that started James down the wrong path. Taking matters into his own hands.

When he was of age, he joined the navy. But he had rheumatic fever when he was a child, which damaged his heart. That cut his navy life short, so when he returned home, that left him with few options. He did find work at a place there in his home town, but the pay wasn't up to what he was hoping for.

But in the meantime he met a woman that would soon be his wife. But he had to work for that.

They were both young, and her mother, a single parent herself, was very strict. But he was persistent. He went by her house, threw his hat into the foyer, and waited. If it came flying back out, he had best leave. But if it stayed, then he was welcome to come in.

Well, that started a romance that would last a lifetime. They were married and stayed together through thick and thin.

That union produced six kids—four boys and two girls. I am one of the girls here to tell the story of a man with a strong love for his family. He was a proud man with a strong work ethic. He didn't believe in handouts. He believed a man should work for what he had. He believed in God, faith and freedom, and loved his country.

Love and friendship had no bounds. He was glad to help his neighbor, whoever they were. Even strangers benefited from his good nature. Well, that is, until someone crosses him. To be on his side was a better place to be. I'm saying these things because he was my dad, and I witnessed all these things. And I want to preserve his memory and his legacy.

Although he was not a perfect man and he made his living outside the law, it was for his love of family. Sometimes we do the wrong things for the right reasons.

It was apparent that James's mom failed to lead him down the right path, so she would try to put the fear of God in his children. She would come by on Sunday mornings to take us to church. I would always look for ways to get out of it, but they never worked.

She was so persistent. And Dad, well, he said it couldn't hurt. He was sure we would need it. So one Sunday morning came, and sitting beside my grandmother, my brother got up and went down to the front of the church. My big brother was my hero, so I followed him. We asked Jesus to come into our lives, and we were baptized. Our grandmother was so proud that we did that in front of her little church group. The day we were baptized, we came out of that water, but we were still dirty. I believed Jesus had his work cut out for him to clean us up.

At that time, we lived beside some railroad tracks. But I seldom see a rain. I think I recall seeing one. On the other side of those tracks were woods and swamps. A perfect place for a still. Yeah, Dad was in the moonshine business. It was a good place for a still 'cause no one in their right mind would go out there if you didn't know the area. People were known to get lost in the swamps and surely did not want to be in there at night.

After dark, strange sounds came from the woods. Don't go without a gun, for sure. Coyotes, bobcats, bad-boy snakes, and even panthers have been spotted. The scariest sound is that of the dreaded barn owl. You think someone was dying.

Only the brave goes in there at night. LOL (I have seen some grown men running out of there). But Dad wasn't afraid of any of that. He would take his old floppy-ear dog and us and go.

We hunted small game and deer, but our grandparents lived off the land. You never knew what you would find. One day, I happened to go out on the back porch. Pop, our grandfather, said, "Don't touch the wash tub." Well, I had to touch the wash tub, but when I did, something inside moved and scratched. I didn't think any more about it until the next day, when I found an opossum's tail nailed to a tree and a big pot of something boiling on the stove.

There was not enough sweet tea in Tennessee to get me to stay for dinner that night.

Well, it was fall, and Pop and Dad had killed a hog. They were cutting it up to salt it down to cure it in the smokehouse. It was all laid out on the kitchen table. Since it was a cool day, they had the doors open as they went from the kitchen to the smokehouse.

All of a sudden, there was a growl at the door. Pop turned to find a bobcat. He smelled the fresh meat and had come for dinner. Pop had left his gun by the door. He couldn't grab it in time to shoot the cat. But there was a broom leaning against the kitchen chair.

As Mom threw her arms out to push us into the next room, Pop grabbed the broom just as the cat jumped on the table. He slapped that cat from the table to the refrigerator, from the kitchen sink to the stove. Well, the cat gave up and ran back to the swamp. It wasn't too hungry after all, or he was just tired of fighting with Pop. I believe if the devil had walked through that door, Pop would have slapped him with that broom.

I'll never forget the day my brother died. Some friends of the family came over to have dinner and visit. Us kids were outside playing, and Mom and Dad were entertaining their friends. Everyone had finished eating. I was a little late coming to the dinner table. As I was coming in, I happened to look out over the field next to our house. My brother and his friend were crossing over to get to the pond on the other side. He and Dad would often go fishing and frog gigging. Brother loved it, but Dad told him never to go alone.

Well, that day, he went with a friend. I suppose he thought he was not alone. So off they went, two adventurous boys, as boys will do.

The next thing I remember was the sound of police, ambulances, and a recue in the direction of the pond. After a while, police brought Dad to the house. When he got out of the car, Mom ran to him, and they held each other. There were sobs and screams, and Mom fainted in Dad's arms. My brother, my hero, had drowned. I couldn't feel anything; I was numb.

I don't think you really get over the death of a child. Mom was distant; she didn't talk for a long time; she just stared into space.

Dad tried to take care of us the best he could. I always tried to help him. I tried to help along with our grandparents that came.

I would often see my dad cry when he would comb the youngest one's hair. I wondered why God would let this happen.

We would help Dad do the shopping since Mom was out of sorts. Every turn, I was always looking, hoping I'd see my brother 'cause I just couldn't believe he was gone. I can't say what went through Dad's mind at that time, but I think he may have given up on God.

We came alive in the outdoors. Being outside just felt like you were closer to God. After a while, we began to live again. Grief never leaves you, but it will change you. It will make you weaker, or it will make you stronger. Just like the story that the old Indian told his young son about the two wolves. Which one will you feed?

As time went on, Dad started taking us out to the woods. We would take the boat out to the swamps. We would climb in, and Dad would push off from the bank. The water was always muddy, but there was good fishing if you went back into one of the sloughs, usually where the fish would hide.

Noodling was never my thing, but people were there, taking chances. Dad would steer the boat way back in the swamp. He knew all about it, so we had no fears. The only fear was hoping one of the bad boy snakes wasn't going to fall in the boat from a low hanging tree limb.

We would shoot the ones we would see sunning on the bank. That's where we learn to shoot. It was good target practice. At the end of the day, we would always try to find Mom some poke salad. It grew wild, so you had to know what to look for. There was a special process to preparing it, and she loved it; I did not.

On our way home that day, the closer we got, we could see smoke rising in the distance. When we got to our house, or where it used to be, Mom let out a horrible scream. Our house was almost burned to the ground. Everything we had, everything we owned, was gone up in smoke. Just gone. We searched through the ashes to find something worth keeping, but there was no use; it was all gone. We stayed with relatives 'till Dad rebuilt.

For anything that happens, there is always someone somewhere who knows.

Later on, we found out it was a person who was mad at dad for not letting him in on his bootlegging. You can't trust just anyone, and Dad was a pretty good judge of character. Dad couldn't prove that the person was there. There were no witnesses. The person who burned the house knew where the still was, so Dad had to move it to different locations just to be safe. If he went as far as burning down our house, what would they do next?

I think all that happened in our lives as we grew up around these things installed in us a sense of caution that anything can and will happen at any time. We were always on the defensive and grew up really fast.

When we were very young, we never knew when holidays came around except when Mom would cook a big dinner and tell us what we were celebrating. One winter, an aunt on our mother's side came to stay with us for a while. Her children were about the same age as we were. This was after our brother died, and she came to be with Mom at this terrible time.

We didn't know that Christmas would be here until the day we went to cut down that big tree that never fit until Dad trimmed it. We decorated with all sorts of things we had around the house 'cause we couldn't afford the store-bought stuff. We got up one cold morning to hear the other kids laughing and tearing paper off presents. We looked around, but there were no presents under the tree for us. No toys from Santa.

Mom and Dad tried to explain to us that our cousins had to have their Christmas that day because they would be on the road on the real Christmas day.

After our aunt and cousins left, some people came to the house with a big box of different kinds of toys. I didn't think Santa sent people to the front door.

I remember Mom and Dad looking really sad. They tried to hide their feelings, but I could see the sadness in their faces. I don't know if it was the whole Christmas thing or because it was the first Christmas without their firstborn son. Dad made a decision. Things would get better no matter what the cost. There's always a price to pay for everything we do.

Yeah, Dad was in the moonshine business, and he was good at it and made a good living for his family, but it was a risky business. He had a good partner and was friends with some shady characters. We were raised around that, so it didn't feel strange.

Some strange people would come to the house and go to the still with Dad. They would come back to the house and stand around and discuss supplies and deliveries. We could help load the car down with twenty to thirty gallons. And then take off four fifty-five-gallon drums of corn mash to the swamp.

25

Every so often, Mama got her a little taste of the homebrew. The man who owned the grocery store and nightclub was a really good friend. He supplied Dad with what he needed, and Dad paid him with whisky for his bar.

Of course it was a bad part of town. It was so bad the law was never seen there. It got pretty bad sometimes. There was illegal gambling and prostitution. If it was illegal, you could find it there. He had some big bouncers. They were glad to see dad drive up with the brew.

We were always made to stay in the car, but we knew what was going on. But we were James kids, so the bouncers always looked after us.

Now every town had some rough area you just didn't go to, unless, of course, you knew people and they knew you. Places like that settle things their way. You didn't see a lot of law enforcement. They had their own laws. Now Dad has a good relationship with this man. Everyone knew Dad, and he knew most of the people there. Even though everyone knew everyone,

When we went with Dad, we were made to stay in the car with the doors locked. No exceptions. We could see a lot going on just by watching people go to and from the place. We went with him to a lot of places and met a lot of people. Now hands-on for us was strictly forbidden. He tried to shield us from the evils out there, but it just wasn't meant to be. You know what they say about your best laid plans. I guess you could say that when we got older, it was hard for him to keep all of us little ducks in a roll.

There were always a few close calls, but Dad somehow was able to avoid them. One night he was making a delivery to the grocery man or nightclub. We helped load the car and went with him. When he got there, he drove down the alley and blew the horn. A couple of big guys came out to unload the car. Dad followed them back inside and told us to stay in the car and to keep the doors locked.

In a little while, Dad came back out. Just as he was about to get into the car, a man came out of the shadows with a gun.

He had witnessed the transaction and wanted to rob him. Dad always carried brass knuckles and a pistol in his pocket. But before he could reach for them, the men that helped him came out of the building. One shot into the air, and the mugger ran off.

We over heard a conversation between Dad and the two men. One said, "We know the problems you are having with the law, and we can get rid of the sheriff for you. They will never find him, and you won't be involved, we'll take care of it."

Dad said, "That's okay, thanks for the offer. I'll take care of it."

Dad had knowledge and associates connected to what was known as the Dixie Mafia.

Now, the place at the state line was notorious for illegal gambling and prostitution. If it was illegal, you could find it there.

I went with Dad once. He told me to set in the car and, if he wasn't out in ten minutes, to start the car and drive back. There were men in the parking lot with guns strapped to their hips. I wasn't about to leave him, so I went inside.

The men at the bar had guns on them. You could tell they were cautious by the way they stared at people that came in the door, cause they stared me down pretty good. It was obvious I was underage.

Before Dad came from the back, there was a ruckus at one of the gambling tables. A man got up swinging, and two other men jumped up, beat the man down, and drug him out the back door. Dad had conducted his business there, and we were on our way home. Dad said, "I don't want to ever find you in one of those places." I didn't say anything on the way home.

Dad wasn't much of a drinking man, but he loved the money. He wanted a better life for us. But it was going to take the hand of God or maybe the devil to take us away from all that.

Dad's moonshine kept him busy and on the road a lot. Mom tried to keep the house and kids in order, which was a job all by itself. Dad had gone out of town and was gone for a while. Mom asked her brother to go into town with her. I don't know if she was suspicious of Dad cause he had been gone for some time or if she was just tired of running the house and kids all by herself.

Mom carried a pistol with her since she was alone at home a lot.

As they turned a corner, she could not believe her eyes. Her husband, the love of her life, was helping some other woman in a car. Her mind went in all different directions. He had left her to take care of his children, and now this! Her emotions got the best of her. She pulled out the gun and shot. Fortunately, she was a bad shot.

Her brother grabbed the gun, and Dad came running over and grabbed her. Well, after the dust settled, Dad explained to Mom that it was a woman who owned a nightclub at the state line and wanted to talk to him about bringing some shine to her place.

More often than not, since I was the oldest, whenever Mom and Dad would leave the house, they would leave me in charge.

One day, my siblings were riding their bikes up and down the driveway. All of a sudden, a man came racing into the driveway.

Obviously looking for Dad. I believed the man was drunk or just crazy. He jumped from the car, waving his arms and cussing, calling the kids some awful names. I ran outside, amazed at what this man was doing. Well, I had enough, I started saying some things we were told not to say. Dad was very strict. We were not to drink, smoke, or cuss. His favorite line was "Don't do what I do. Do what I say." Well, I forgot all that. I started calling that man every bad word in the English language, some of which he may not have heard before.

He lunged toward me, and I lunged back. I wasn't about to back down. I think we all had Dad's temper. He finally left. It wasn't long after Mom and Dad returned home. Of course, my brothers couldn't wait to tell them. Dad told me to sit; and he, along with Mom went to pay this man a visit. Little brother stayed behind, looked at me, and said in his most southern drawl, "You about to get your ass whopped." I sat and waited for my punishment for cussing. But to my surprise, Dad came in, looked at me, and said,

"Don't be cussing." I just had to look at my little brother and just smile and wink.

There was a man in the area who was just cruel. Dad didn't like the man, but he treated him with respect. Dad was just that way. He happened to be dating Dad's aunt. Dad went to visit her one day. She was so bruised. He finally got her to tell him what happened. Her friend had hit her across the face with a sack of nails. Dad saw red. He went home, loaded his gun, and went to the man's house. He kicked the door open (when he came after you, he didn't bother knocking on the door). He put the gun in the man's face and was about to pull the trigger when his aunt jumped between them. She begged Dad not to shoot him; he was not worth going to prison for.

Instead, Dad hit the man with the butt end of the gun and told him he would kill him if it happened again. And even if his dog comes up missing, he would be back to kill him, and no one would ever find his body.

I never heard about the man after that day, so I can't say what happened to him—if he left on his own or not.

Cause Dad had such a reputation, he had a few enemies. He was very careful about when he went to the still. And always looking over his shoulder. I think his actions also taught us to be cautious as well. As kids, we grew up fast and learned a lot more about life than other kids.

Dad and mom left one day to take a few pints of whiskey to a customer. They took my little brother along since it was a short trip.

The law knew Dad and what he was into, so whenever they saw him out, they would always try to stop him. That day would be no different. A couple of rookie cops saw Dad, and the chase was on.

Mom started throwing the whiskey bottles out the car window and breaking them on the street. Of course, Dad wasn't stopping, so they shot out the front tire, causing him to hit a pole.

Now that the whiskey was splattered all over the street, they couldn't arrest Dad. There was no evident problem, but there was a bigger problem. All through this, little brother was thrown all over the car. There was a big gash on his head and blood everywhere. Mom was hysterical; they were trying to arrest Dad, but one cop had enough sense to realize they needed to get them to a doctor. Police endangering a child did not look good on the department. Dad had a really good lawyer.

How that was settled—I won't be talking about that here.

Since I was the oldest, I did help out around the house. Mom had an old ringer-type washer. One day, she asked me to take the clothes out and hang them on the line. Well, my little sister was always following me. That day, when no one was looking, I lit up a cigarette. Now, my little sister was scared of her own shadow. She began to cry and say, "You're going to get in trouble."

"I won't if you shut up." But she kept on and on. And in the commotion, my hair got caught around the ringer and started pulling it around.

Well, since my hair was really long about my waist, I didn't notice; but when I realized what happened, I simply hit the lever, and it opened up enough so I could pull it out. I threw the cigarette down and chased her until she ran behind Mom.

Later on, she said she didn't want me to get in trouble and wouldn't tell if I told her about my boyfriend. I was only fourteen at the time. I didn't have a boyfriend, but I made up stories, and she would laugh. And life was good again for a while.

But good times don't last forever.

That year, I started high school. It was not a good time for me. Trying to fit in was awkward. New school, new teachers, and new friends. I did my best to make friends and fit in, but gossip travels faster than wildfire. Kids can be so cruel. Dad's reputation had followed us to school. We were shamed and talked about behind our backs, not to our faces, but we could hear the whispers.

I went to bed crying a few times.

Mom and Dad didn't know what was going on at school. I hated school, but Dad was adamant, and school was very important. I took algebra that first year, which turned out to be a big mistake. It was hard for me, and the teacher was no help. When I raised my hand for help, he would just ignore me. Passed over me like I wasn't even sitting there. When he called the roll in the morning, he passed over me. Was I invisible?

Well, I got tired of that, so I just skipped that class and got in trouble for that. I think we were baptized in muddy water.

I began to hang out with a bad crowd of kids. I made friends with a girl who lived down the road. I would lie and tell my parents I was spending the night with her; actually, I was, but we would sneak out of the house and go to bars.

There were bars in the area that knew we were underage but no one cared. While partying at a local bar one night, I happened to walk up to the bar for a drink. Over in the corner, in the shadows, I saw someone I had seen before.

A tall, dark, handsome drink of water that I had seen come to the house before. An associate of Dad's. Oh no, I was caught for sure.

Well, I wasn't about to turn and leave. That would make me look guilty. So my friend and I walked up to the bar. She ordered a Coke. I ask the bartender for a shot of whiskey. He knew we were underage, but he didn't care. He poured a shot and set it down in front of me. Before I picked it up, the big, burly man leaned over the bar stared at me, and said, "Baby girl, if you woman enough to drink this, you smile."

I wasn't about to back down. I turned that glass up and downed it in one big swallow. I looked up at him and smiled really pretty. He turned to another customer. I looked at my friend, and she knew.

She took my arm and led me outside. As I leaned up against the side of the building, she was trying to pour her coke down me to put out the hellfire that was burning my insides. The man there who knew dad came out, walked by us, and just smiled. Thankfully, he never told Dad we were there.

Making it and hauling it was one thing,

I found out that night that drinking straight whiskey was not for me.

I never saw my dad take a drink of whiskey. If they had friends over for card games, he might drink a beer.

But his moonshine whiskey was all business.

One weekend, I went over to my friend's house. We were going out that night, but of course my parents didn't know our plans. After a night of parties, we were driving back to her house.

Well she was driving. We were laughing and talking about what a good time we had. Thinking back, I think she had a little too much to drink. All of a sudden, blue lights were flashing behind us. She said, "Let's make a run for it." I told her she had lost her mind and to pull over. The officer came to the window and asked for her driver's license. I don't know why they do that. He knew we had been drinking and were now driving. He was the cop that came into the bar when we were there and also knew we were underage.

Well, he took us in. All I could think about was hoping Dad didn't find out. Now I don't know if the sheriff felt sorry for us, or maybe he knew my dad. But whatever the case, he said, "Now girls, I know you'll be out just fooling around tonight, so I tell you what, if you can call someone to come pick you up, you can leave." We had a sigh of relief. But who should I call? So I thought maybe Dad's friend was still at the bar. And I hoping just that maybe he would bring someone with him to drive her car back.

We were just out having a good time, but we didn't know all the trouble we could have gotten into. Because the deputy was trying really hard to get us back in the cell.

So I called the bar, hoping he was still there. Lucky for me, he was. I told him where I was and asked if he would come get me. I explained that we could leave if someone came to get us. And I wasn't about to call Dad. I could hear him almost laughing and said, "He'd be there in a bit."

So I sat my butt on the corner of the sheriff's desk,

winked at the deputy, and waited. I was so happy to see that man walk through the door. He asked where we wanted to go. My friend's house, of course, wasn't going home.

I tried not to look at him. He was so handsome, with dark hair and deep brown eyes that seemed to look right into your soul.

He parked ways from the house so we could walk the rest of the way so no one would hear us coming in. He said, "Careful, girls, some men might take advantage of this situation."

He was so nice, throwing that big smile at me and saying he would wait there until we got inside.

When I got home the next morning, the sheriff's car and some black cars and men all dressed in black were in the yard. Later, I found out they were federal marshals.

I thought for sure I was in trouble and that the sheriff was telling dad about my incident. But how is all this for me? As I tried to walk by unnoticed, I overheard one say,

"James, we got a tip that someone was operating a still in the area."

Dad replied, "Don't know anything about that."

The man asked again, "You sure, 'cause our sources were pretty adamant with their statement."

Dad, with his sarcastic attitude and tired of all the questions, calmly said, "Do your ears work, or are they just for show?"

The man looked a little puzzled. Then Dad said, "Let me call someone who can help you here." Dad called his lawyer.

If you were caught red-handed with something, he'd get you out of it. He worked for some high-profile people. Which we won't be mentioning here.

When dad's lawyer got there, he asked what the problem was. The federal man who had been talking to dad explained what they were doing. The lawyer told the officers that if they didn't have a warrant for anything, they needed to leave. He said, "You are harassing and causing embarrassment to this man and his family. This man is a pillow in this community. His children have to go to school here. Do you know what your presence is doing to them? Unless you have some hard evidence for being here, we're done here."

A few weeks later, on a school trip, the kids in the back of the bus were getting rowdy. They put a girl up talking smack to me. I tried to ignore her, but they wouldn't stop. As I got up to get off the bus, she grabbed my hair and pulled me almost to the floor. Everyone was laughing. I got my footing and came back with a slap across her face. They weren't laughing any more. The bigger kids reached for her, and the bus driver stopped the bus and grabbed me. Of course, I was expelled from riding the bus for a few days. and that was fine with me.

59

Summer was finally here. No more bad teachers and mean kids to put up with.

But I did learn algebra that summer. I went to the library, checked out books, and taught myself.

I also got my driver's license that summer. After begging my dad to let me drive one day, he tossed me the keys. I backed out and drove down to church. I turned to come back and hit the preacher's mailbox. I was so scared when I got home. The preacher had called my dad, and he was on his way to set it back up.

Late one night, we loaded the car with about thirty gallons. He took the back seat out so that many would fit easily. He headed out before daylight and got to the river. He had a flat, and since he didn't have room for a spare, we took one to him. We carefully transferred the whiskey from one car to the other. As he was changing the tire, a cop stopped and asked if he needed help. Dad said we were fine. The man drove off, and he avoided an arrest again.

Fall was here, and school started back. Not a real bonus, but I went to the library, and I had learned algebra on my own just to prove to myself I could do it.

Winter was on the way—not my favorite time of year. All the cold, rain, and snow. Snow was rare, but it happened.

At Christmas, we went to the woods to pick out our tree. It always looked small until we got it to the house, then had to cut the top out to make it fit because it was so big. It was a tradition to go to all that trouble, but it always turned out beautiful.

We saved enough money and bought Dad a pair of house shoes. We were so excited, and he was really surprised when he opened that box.

We were opening presents and eating a Christmas breakfast when we heard it. Some kind of explosion. We all jumped and ran to the door. Dad ran ahead of us 'cause he knew what had happened. There was a malfunction; the still exploded. We could hear the glass jugs breaking and the fire cracking. Dad finally got things under control and came back to the house.

He was wearing the house shoes, but they were ruined. Apparently, they weren't rainproof. Dad felt bad about the shoes, but it couldn't be helped.

We would take out the back seat to make room and put blocks in the springs so the car wouldn't set low. Late one night, we loaded the car with about thirty gallons. Dad was leaving early before daylight the next morning for a delivery. The kids ask to go. Dad didn't see the harm. It would give them some time together.

Everything was fine when they crossed the state line. Dad began to cough, and the car weaved a little. Just so happened, a highway patrol was setting off to the side and started to follow.

He knew he didn't need to get stopped, so he sped up a little. The officer came after him, and the chase was on. There had been a few bootleggers in the area, so the officer knew what he had. Dad wouldn't stop. Apparently the officer didn't see the kids in the car and shot at the driver window. Dad's car was pretty souped-up. He managed to get far ahead and pull down a gravel road. He lost the cop, but he was bleeding. The bullet had grazed his arm pretty badly and could not drive. They set out for a spell. Dad told the kids they would have to drive. They had never driven before but would try.

As they started to drive, the car began to slide down a hill. The road was between two lakes. They managed to stop before it hit water. They couldn't drive out, so they ran up to a house to see if someone could pull them out. Luckily, a man with a tractor pulled them up to the road. The man noticed my dad bleeding, but Dad told him he was injured when the car went down the hill, but that was fine. Knowing dad needed a doctor, the kids had to drive to a public place for help. They drove several miles and came to a restaurant.

But it was at the bottom of a hill. They had to stand on the brake with both feet but finally came to a stop.

They pulled in, ran inside, and said their dad was sick and asked if someone would call a doctor. People in the restaurant called an ambulance, and of course the police came too.

They went back to the car, and Dad told him not to give the keys to anyone. They were young and didn't understand what was going on at the time; they were just worried about Dad.

Well, the police had their suspicions when they saw the tarp over the back of the car. They could not search it without a warrant or permission. They had no reason for a warrant, so somehow they had to get the keys.

The sheriff in that county was a woman. Her husband was killed by bootleggers. And she swore vengeance on all bootleggers.

Kids hadn't eaten in a while, so she took them to the restaurant and commenced to buy them food and talk to them about their dad, where they lived, and where they were going.

Of course they weren't talking, but as they ate, she managed to get the keys from his coat pocket. They opened the trunk and found the whiskey. They couldn't do anything with Dad at the time he was in the hospital. They contacted Mother. She and a friend went to get the kids.

Dad was charged and arrested. After a short stay in the hospital, he came home. I don't ever remember him going to jail for this. A good lawyer and people in high places?

So I guess money does talk.

70

While dad was recuperating in the hospital, I had the bright idea to help him out. He still had a few gallons left at the still. So I called the friend of my dad. The guy that was at the house several times. The same one that picked me up at the jail. I won't disclose his name here for obvious reasons. But I called and told him about Dad's situation, and that we had a few gallons left, and if he would take them. He said he would, so I went to the car and loaded it like Dad always did. I covered them with a tarp, drove back to the house.

Got one of dad's guns, and headed for the state line. Dad always said not to speed and obey the driving laws so as not to cause attention.

After crossing the state line, I could see lightning in the distance; it was about to pour down rain. I made it to his driveway, turned out the lights, and slowly made my way to his house.

When I got there, I wasn't sure what to do, so I backed up to the front of the house. It had begun to rain; it came down in buckets. I rolled the window down a bit to try to see. All of a sudden,

Someone was at the window. Scared to death, I hit the man in the face with the butt end of the rifle. He fell back. The door opened, and Dad's friend took my arm, took the gun, and pulled me out of the car. I slipped and slid around and fell in the mud, trying to keep my footing, finally got to the door. He told me to stay there, and he went back outside. After a while, he came back in. I was so cold and wet that I was standing by the fireplace, trying to get warm and dry. He was a little sarcastic. "Don't sit on my couch with those muddy clothes."

He pointed to the bathroom. "You're welcome to use the shower if you want me to wash your clothes."

He went back outside. I don't know why, maybe to move the car. I found out later that he got rid of his drunken friend who showed up unannounced and scared the hell out of me.

Well, I wasn't about to get in that shower. But I did go to the bathroom and wash the mud off my hands and knees. There was a robe on the door, so I put it on to wash the mud out of my clothes in the sink. I cracked open the door and peeked out. I didn't see him, so I went out and hung my clothes over the fireplace to dry.

After a bit, he came back in and set the rifle at the corner of the door. He smiled at me and went into the other room. He came out again, walked over to me, and asked, "You okay?"

Trying not to stare at him, I said, "Yeah."

He stepped closer. "You took a big risk coming here."

I said "I've been with Dad on deliveries." He stood there, staring, which really made me nervous. And the storm wasn't letting up. He stoked the fire and said, "I noticed you looking at me whenever I come to your house.

I replied, "Yeah, well, I noticed everybody."

He asked, "You warm?"

I said, "Yeah," as I moved over a bit. As he keeps getting closer, I unknowingly back myself to the wall. There I was, now what?

He moves up against me, those big brown eyes staring into mine, hypnotizing as if he was searching for my soul. Was he waiting for my reaction? The only reaction was that my heart was beating out of my chest. This man was fine. He was taking my breath away; I couldn't breathe. He pressed me against the wall, and one hand went around my waist as he pulled the robe off my shoulder and kissed my neck ever so softly.

I could feel his breath on my cheek as his lips searched for mine. I managed to say, "I never."

He whispered, "I know." And this time his kiss was so intense that his hand found the opening of the robe and was touching my thigh. Was this the devil that I had heard about pulling me into his tangled web that I couldn't escape from? Soon, the sound of the thunder faded. All I could hear was the sound of my heart beating in my ears as I fell deeper into his web.

It was around midnight. I had to get home. I couldn't let anyone know I had been there. I sneaked out of the house; he didn't
know when I left. I just wanted to go crawl into my bed and pretend
that night never happened.

Ways down the road, I noticed a car following awfully close. If
I sped up, they would speed up. If I passed a car, they passed a car.
This was a little strange. So I speeded up. I thought if I was stopped
for speeding, at least I could complain to the officers that someone
was following me.

I got home, turned out the lights, and pulled around the back of the house. I ran inside and grabbed one of my dad's guns. I peered out the window. The other car turned off their lights and drove past the house really slowly. Someone fired a gun! It scared me to death! What the hell was this? Who was this? Why were they coming after me? I was up all night, afraid they might come back. But I never saw the car again. I don't think they knew me. Did they know Dad? Were they watching Dad's partner and saw me leave his house?

After Dad got home from the hospital, his partner came to see him. When he thought Dad wasn't close enough to hear, he would smile and say, "Hi."

He also said his drunken friend was found dead in his truck. He had been shot. Of course there were no witnesses. There never are.

I told him someone followed me home that night. I said, "Please be careful."

He looked shocked and worried. "What?" He blurted out. "Who was it? I'll kill 'em."

I said, "I don't know. Shh, you're getting loud. Dad will hear you."

He said, "Anytime you need me, I'll be there. Call me."

It was summer and nothing going was on, so Sis and I begged to go with Dad. He was going to the state line bar to talk to the owner. When we got there, the parking lot was full of bikers. They had to stop in for drinks on that hot summer day.

Dad told us to stay in the car and keep the doors locked while he was inside. Well, he took so long that we thought we would sneak in and just stand at the end of the bar unnoticed.

That didn't last long.

One of the bikers came up to us and asked if he could buy us something to drink. I said, "No, we're just waiting for someone." Well, here comes the biker's girlfriend. She was all tattooed and skanky, looking like she was dragged behind the bike instead of riding it. The beer must have been talking for her 'cause she accused us of flirting with her man. I tried to explain, but she wasn't having it.

She grabbed my sister's hair. Oh, hell no, that was the wrong thing to do.

Sister reached and grabbed the girl's earring and yanked it out of her ear. The whole crowd was in a scuffle. With all the drinking, it didn't take much to set this bunch off. Dad and the owner of the place heard the ruckus came from the back room, both with their guns to their sides. Dad managed to shove us out the door and into the car.

We got a good chewing out all the way home. He was so mad at us. He said I've told ya'll so many times don't do what I do, do what I tell you to do.

We were in hot water for a long time after that.

Whiskey sales were good. Life was good. We get so caught up in life that we fail to stop looking around and appreciate everything God has blessed us with. And it's so sad that in a moment of time, without warning, your whole life can change forever. Everything you've ever known is ripped out of your life.

Dad's partner came to the house one day. They left to go see a potential buyer. It was a cold January day. It was raining and was beginning to mix with a little snow.

I was helping mom clean up after supper when we heard a loud commotion. We ran outside to see another car run Dad's car into the bank. Dad jumped out with his gun and got a shot off through the side window of the other car. But he was shot, and he fell back into the car.

His partner got out and tried to get a shot off, but he wasn't fast enough. He took a shotgun blast to the chest and fell back. As the other car sped off, all we could see were taillights in the dark.

We ran to them screaming, crying, and falling around in the mud and snow. But we were helpless. We cried out to God for help. But help didn't come.

A piece of us died that night. An investigation was done, but as usual, the police were useless. Everyone knew what Dad was doing. The law was always after him anyway. Someone somewhere knows all too well what happened that night and where the responsibility lies. But the truth will never be told.

William Shakespeare once said, "There are two important days in one's life. The day you were born and the day you find out why."

People talked about the day I was born. People will talk about the day I die. But I get to talk about the days in between.

When we come up out of that muddy water through life, we still feel as if we're fighting and clawing our way through all that mud. Even though it will take a lifetime.

Jesus will clean us up.

About the Author

SHE WAS BORN and raised in the southern part of the US. Growing up in a culture of lawlessness, she was compelled to write her stories of hopes and dreams and struggles and triumphs. She hopes to encourage her readers that no matter how you start out in life, you can still do great things.